Down,
  down
  in the depths
    of the sunless sea,
      deep,
        deep
        in the cold,
          cold dark,
            creatures,
            strange
              and fearsome,
                lurk.

and ghostly, lidless eyes
    they glide;
        some large as buses,
            some weighing a ton.
So big, yet rarely seen.
Instead, they are merely glimpsed,
    now and then,
        from the prow of a ship . . .
            from a rocky seashore . . .
                through the lens of an underwater camera.
Who are these giants of the dark seas?
How do they hunt?
How do they eat?
How do they breed?

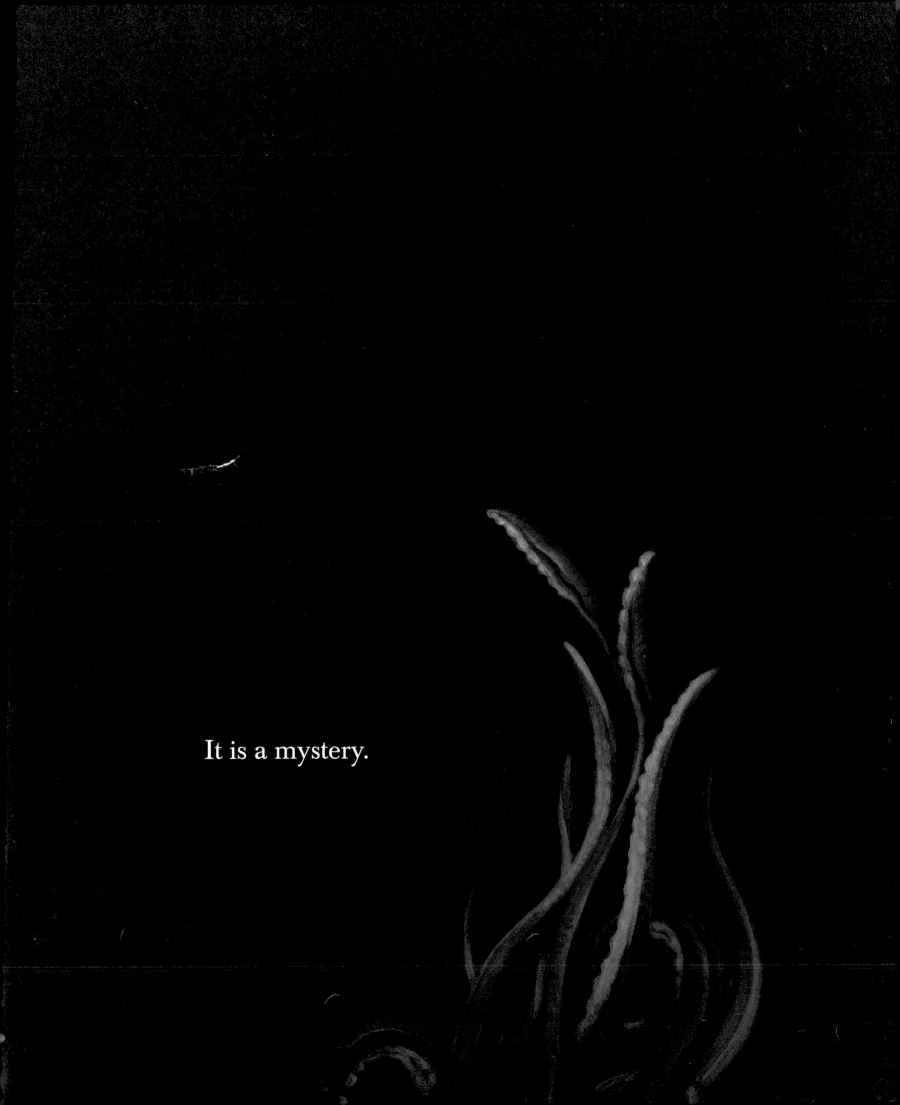

It is a mystery.

After all, how can you know
about an animal hidden from view?
You must rely on clues,
        as scientists do,
                clues left behind
                        by the creatures themselves.
A tentacle.
An eye.
Pieces found around the world,
        found over centuries,
                by whalers,
                        and sailors,
                                and people walking the beach.
You examine each piece,
        questioning and guessing,
                wondering at the weirdness
                        of these baffling beasts.

Beasts we call . . .

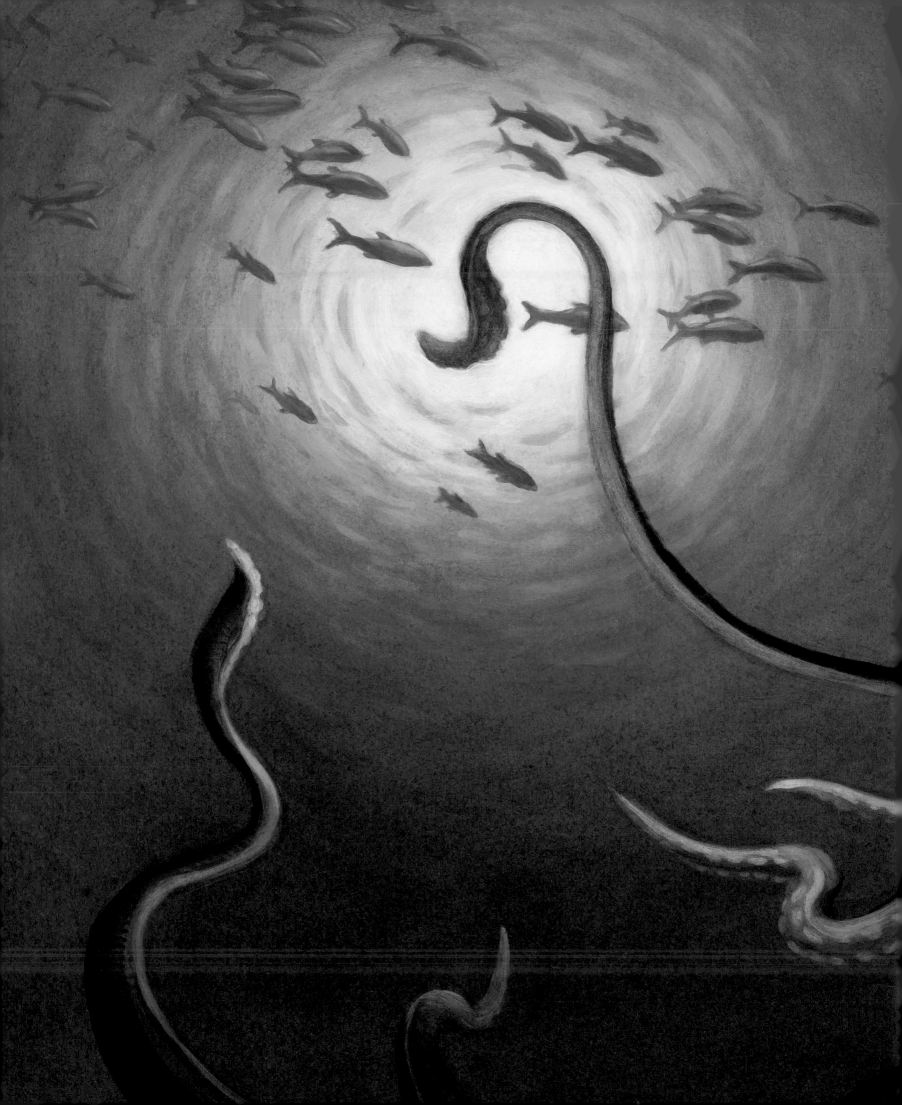

GIANT SQUID

CANDACE FLEMING   ERIC ROHMANN

A NEAL PORTER BOOK
ROARING BROOK PRESS
NEW YORK

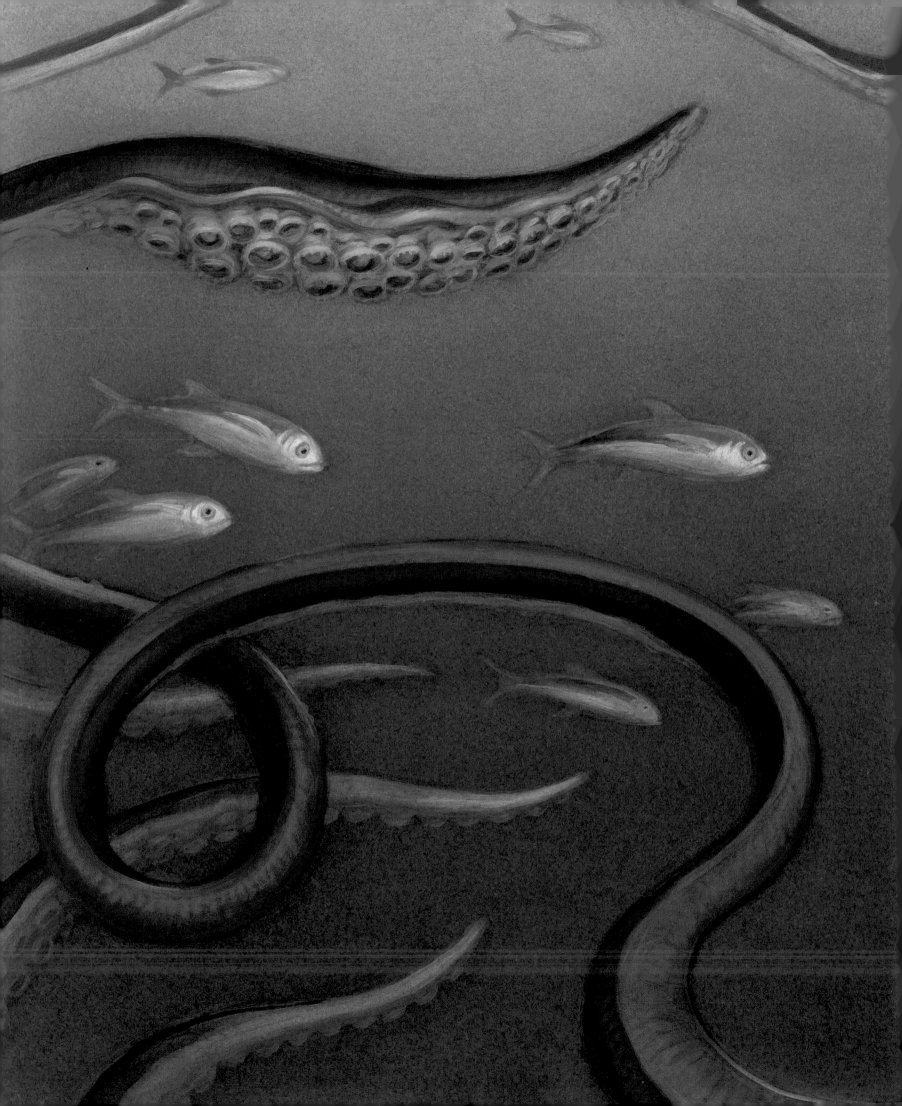

Here are its tentacles,
two,
    curling and twisting and thirty feet long,
      waiting for–
        a passing fish . . .
         another squid . . .
anything swimming by.

The tentacles seize their prey.
They surround their thrashing meal.
They latch on with powerful
sucker-studded clubs.
Row after row of suckers.
Suckers ringed with saw-like teeth
that rip into skin and hold on tight.
Eight coiling arms join in,
pushing the prey to its beak.

The beak.
Bone-hard and parrot-like,
    it sits in the center of those eight,
        slithering arms,
protruding from the creature's mouth,
rotating from side to side,
ripping apart prey.

And what lies behind the beak?
A dark hole . . .
    the mouth.
And inside the mouth?
A terrifying tongue-like ribbon of muscle
covered with sharp, tiny blades that
    slice…
        grind…
file the food into a pasty sludge
easy for giant squid to digest.

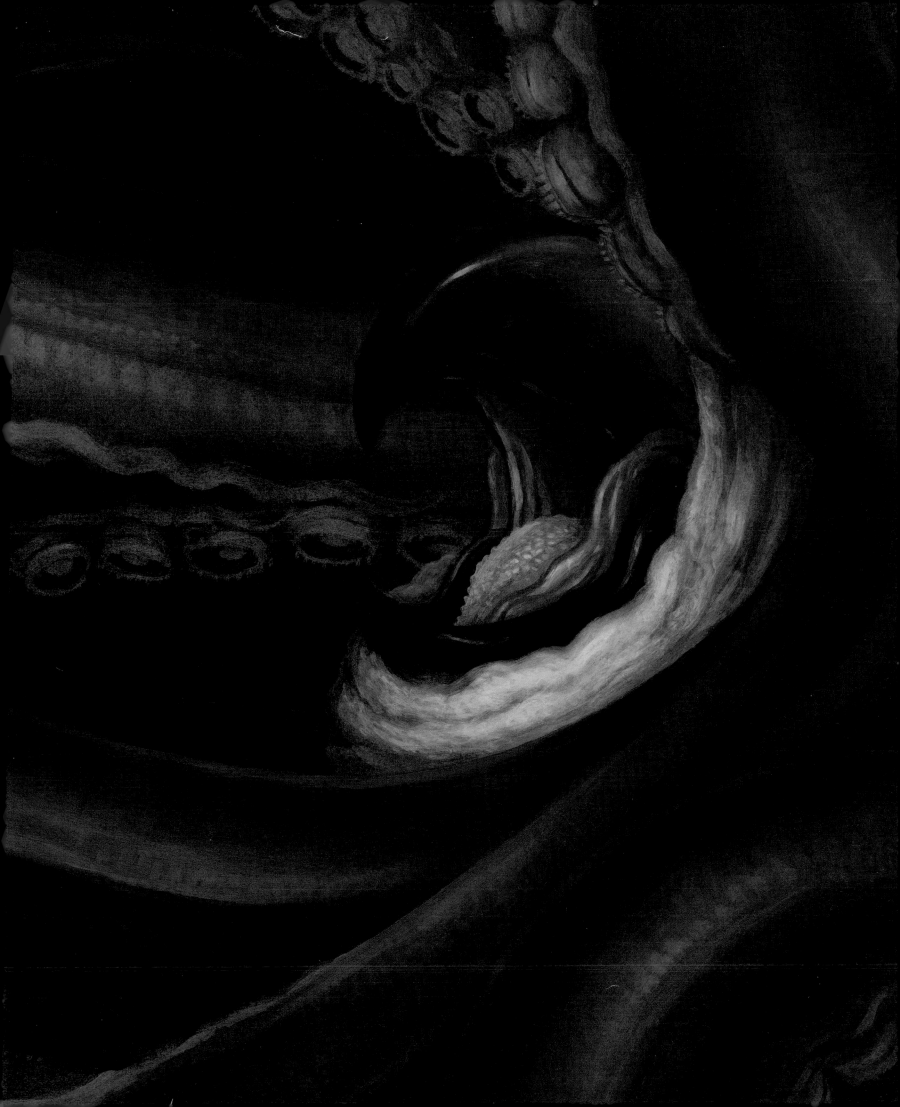

In the murk . . . an eye!
Round.
Unblinking.
Some as big as soccer balls.
The biggest eyes on the planet.
Why?

So it can spy pinpoints of light in its
pitch-black world.
   Glints.
     Flickers.
Set off by tiny creatures—
   jellyfish and krill—
     disturbed by a diving sperm whale.
Their flashes create a shimmering outline.
   Faint.
     So faint.

But not too faint for the big-eyed squid.
The outline is a warning.
Time to flee!
Sucking water into its body, and squirting it out—

the creature jets away.

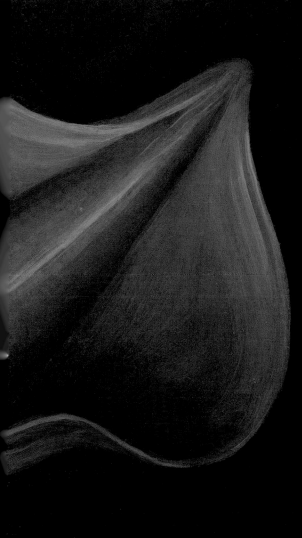

Danger past,
    alone once more in the murky depths,
        the creature floats,
            rising and falling at will.
The squid is pinkish purple now,
but any second it could change color.
Maybe pale yellow.
Maybe silvery gray.
Maybe red with brown stripes
    or orange with black dots.
Which colors?
    Which patterns?
It's another mystery.

And why do they change?
Maybe to impress a mate.

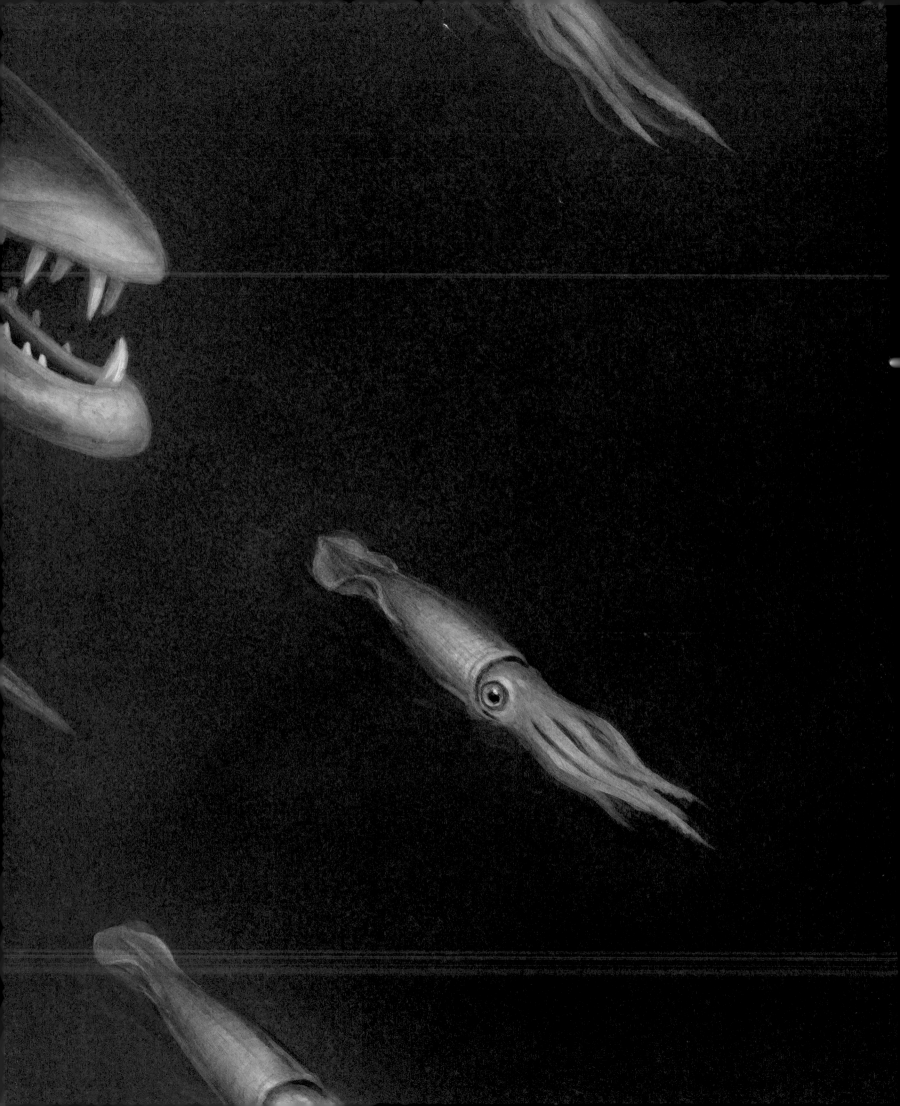

Where does the female squid lay her eggs?
How long does it take them to hatch?
More unanswered questions.
Still more mystery.
Yet one day a baby giant squid
hatches from its egg.
Teensy.
Tiny.
Just two inches long.
In the ocean
it is dangerous to be bite-sized.

Watch out for that barracuda!
Quick!

continue to ask. Since the giant squid has never been studied in its natural habitat, no one has ever seen it hunt or eat until 2012 or reproduce ever. How they carry out these most basic behaviors is guesswork. And they aren't the only unanswered questions. How long do giant squid live? How big can they grow? Do they live in schools? Are they fast swimmers? How far down can they swim?

The questions go on.

Scientists keep searching for answers.

And the giant squid glides through the deep—still elusive, still mysterious, and still keeping its secrets.

BIBLIOGRAPHY

Dery, Mark. "The Kraken Wakes: What *Architeuthis* is Trying to Tell Us." Accessed April 12, 2013. Boingboing.net/2013/01/28/the-kraken-awakes-what-ar.html.

Ellis, Richard. *Monsters of the Sea: The History, Natural History and Mythology of the Oceans' Most Fantastic Creatures.* Guilford, CT: The Lyons Press, 2006.

Ellis, Richard. *The Search for the Giant Squid: The Biology and Mythology of the World's Most Elusive Sea Creature.* New York: Penguin Books, 1999.

Frank, Matthew Gavin. *Preparing the Ghost: An Essay Concerning the Giant Squid and Its First Photographer.* New York: Liveright Publishing Corporation, 2014.

Grann, David. "The Squid Hunter." *The New Yorker*, May 24, 2004. Accessed April 12, 2013. newyorker.com/magazine/2004/05/24/the-squid-hunter.

Switek, Brian. "The Giant Squid: Dragon of the Deep." *Smithsonian Magazine*, June 21, 2011. Accessed April 12, 2013. smithsonianmag.com/science-nature/the-giant-squid-dragon-of-the-deep-18784038/

Williams, Wendy. *Kraken: The Curious, Exciting and Slightly Disturbing Science of Squid.* New York: Abrams Image, 2011.

ACKNOWLEDGMENTS

I am especially grateful to Dr. Edith Widder of ORCA (Ocean Research & Conservation Association), marine biologist, deep-sea explorer, and bioluminescence expert for sharing her time, expertise, and enthusiasm for the giant squid by fact-checking this book. I am also obliged to Richard Ellis, author of *The Search for the Giant Squid*, who helpfully answered my squid questions.

SEARCHING FOR GIANT SQUID ONLINE

There are plenty of places to search for giant squid online. Here are a few of my favorite sites:

See Dr. Edith Widder's first-ever film footage of a giant squid in the wild. Click on other links to see more incredible squid discoveries made by the scientists on her expedition. discovery.com/tv-shows/curiosity/videos/first-video-of-a-giant-squid.htm

See the 2015 encounter. cnn.com/2015/12/28/asia/toyama-japan-giant-squid/

Sponsored by the National Museum of Natural History, this site covers everything from giant squid anatomy to the history of squid science. ocean.si.edu/giant-squid

Watch scientists in action as they dissect and examine the almost-intact body of a giant squid that washed up on a New Zealand beach. new.livestream.com/accounts/5183627/events/3069649?query=&cat=event

An interactive site that allows you to discover giant squid through activities, scientific investigations and formulation of your own plan to uncover the animal's secrets. teacher.scholastic.com/activities/explorations/squid/

OTHER BOOKS ABOUT GIANT SQUID

Cerullo, Mary. *Searching for a Sea Monster.* New York: Capstone Press, 2012.

Dussling, Jennifer. *Giant Squid: Mystery of the Deep.* New York: Penguin Young Readers, 1999.

Newquist, HP. *Here There Be Monsters: The Legendary Kraken and the Giant Squid.* Boston: Houghton Mifflin Harcourt, 2010.

Redmond, Shirley Raye. *Tentacles!: Tales of the Giant Squid.* New York: Random House Books for Young Readers, 2003.

To Scott and Samantha

Text copyright © 2016 by Candace Fleming

Illustrations copyright © 2016 by Eric Rohmann

A Neal Porter Book

Published by Roaring Brook Press

Roaring Brook Press is a division of Holtzbrinck Publishing Holdings Limited Partnership

175 Fifth Avenue, New York, New York 10010

The art for this book was created using oil paint on paper.

mackids.com

Library of Congress Cataloging-in-Publication Data

Names: Fleming, Candace, author. | Rohmann, Eric, illustrator.

Title: Giant squid / by Candace Fleming ; illustrated by Eric Rohmann.

Description: First edition. | New York : Roaring Brook Press, 2016. | "A Neal
   Porter Book." | Audience: Ages 6–10.

Identifiers: LCCN 2015038610 | ISBN 9781596435995 (hardcover)

Subjects: LCSH: Giant squids–Juvenile literature.

Classification: LCC QL430.3.A73 F54 2016 | DDC 594/.58–dc23

LC record available at http://lccn.loc.gov/2015038610

Our books may be purchased in bulk for promotional, educational, or business use. Please
contact your local bookseller or the Macmillan Corporate and Premium Sales Department
at (800) 221-7945 ext. 5442 or by e-mail at MacmillanSpecialMarkets@macmillan.com.

First edition 2016

Printed in China by Toppan Leefung Printing Ltd., Dongguan City, Guangdong Province

1   3   5   7   9   10   8   6   4   2

THE MYSTERIOUS GIANT SQUID

For as long as people have sailed the seas, they have searched for the giant squid. Early mariners were the first to keep an eye out for the creature. Again and again, they told tales of a fearsome sea monster with thick arms, huge, unblinking eyes, and a bird-like beak. Nowadays, we recognize these "monsters" as giant squid. But in many ways—despite scientific and technological advances—the creature remains a mystery.

Incredibly, we have more close-up photos of the surface of Mars—a planet millions of miles away—than we have of giant squid. We know more about the behavior of dinosaurs—extinct for 65 million years—than we do a creature that resides in almost all the world's oceans and is one of the biggest animals on the planet. So elusive is the giant squid that the first time scientists ever saw a living one was in 2006. Since then, we've gotten a few more glimpses. In 2012 scientists captured brief film footage of one swimming in the cold, dark depths of the Pacific Ocean, 2,066 feet below the surface. And in 2015 a giant squid appeared in a Japanese harbor where it swam for several hours, allowing spectators and divers a rare, close-up encounter.

So how do we know about these mysterious creatures? From the bits and pieces of them discovered on the ocean's surface or washed up on the world's beaches. While in some rare cases people discovered an intact carcass, most of these specimens lacked heads or bodies. Some were just a tentacle or an eye. Others were nothing more than a sucker. Scientists examined each of these pieces. They dissected, described, and detailed them. They even gave the creature a scientific name, *Architeuthis* (pronounced arc-eh-tooth-is), in Latin, meaning "ruling squid." Slowly, over the course of decades, these bits of evidence led to bits of knowledge.

And what strange bits of knowledge they are! Imagine scientists' astonishment when they cut through the mantle of a giant squid to discover that the creature's esophagus (the tube leading from mouth to stomach) runs directly through its brain. Or that a special sac located at the end of its digestive system makes and stores a thick, dark ink that can be ejected at will. Or that the giant squid has not one . . . not two . . . but *three* hearts, pumping blood—*blue* blood—to every part of its body. But these findings are just the beginning. That's why every specimen is precious.

Some of the best squid specimens have been found inside sperm whales. Growing to a length of 60 feet, sperm whales routinely dive for more than an hour to depths of 3,280 feet in search of their favorite meal—giant squid. Down in the darkness of the deep ocean, the whale cannot see its prey. Instead it uses echolocation, producing a series of loud clicks that travel through the water and bounce off objects. The reflected sound bounces back and the whale interprets it, determining the size and whereabouts of prey.

No one has ever seen an encounter between a sperm whale and a giant squid. But since giant squid can grow to be 30 feet or longer (the biggest one ever recorded by scientists reached almost 43 feet) *Architeuthis* is big enough to fight back. It's clear from sucker scars often found on sperm whales that the battles are vicious. Sometimes the squid escapes. More often, the whale wins. Grabbing its meal with its teeth, it gulps it down whole.

When sperm whales are caught by fisherman or wash up on beaches, parts of giant squid are found in the their stomachs—arms, tentacles, and beaks. A lot of beaks. Sometimes as many as 5,000 to 7,000 per whale! Sperm whales are unable to digest these beaks, made of a hard substance named chitin. Some scientists believe so many beaks can mean just one thing—there are *millions* of giant squid swimming in the ocean. Millions! So why haven't we encountered them more often?

That is just one of the many questions scientists

BEAK Located in the middle of the corona of arms, made of a hard substance and as big as a grapefruit, the beak can both rotate and protrude. The upper part of the beak has a downward point making it the perfect cutting edge, while the lower beak rips the food into grape-sized pieces

ARMS Extending down from around the giant squid's mouth, its eight arms—each up to 9.8 feet long—are made entirely of muscle. From base to tip, the inner surface of each is covered with suckers—as many as 300 per arm. They are as big as 2 inches in diameter, each sucker contains a ring of razor-sharp chitin.

TENTACLES Reaching lengths of 33 to 40 feet, these two appendages are smooth from their base to near their end where they expand to resemble a club. Along the tentacle club runs a series of suckers and bumps. Because the opposite tentacle club has the same exact pattern, a sort of zipper effect is created, allowing giant squid to lock its two tentacles together. This gives the animal extra strength and stability when catching prey.

FINS Running partway down the side of the mantle are two stabilizing fins. They are used for balance and maneuverability as it moves through the water.

MANTLE The mantle is a big ring of muscle containing all the animal's respiratory, circulatory, reproductive, and digestive organs. When the giant squid wants to move quickly, it relaxes the muscles in the mantle wall, allowing water to flow into the mantle cavity through special flaps located on either side of its head. Then it contracts the mantle muscles, closing the flaps and forcing water out of the funnel.

FUNNEL Located between the head and the mantle, the funnel functions a bit like a rudder. It can be aimed in any direction, allowing the giant squid to propel through the water—forward, backward, side-to-side, and up and down.

EYES Located one on either side of its head, the giant squid's eyes are the biggest in the animal kingdom. Some can even grown as large as 10 inches in diameter—the size of a human head. Scientists think this big size allows giant squid to see tiny pricks of light produced by other marine creatures (called bioluminescence) or perhaps the silhouettes of predatory sperm whales.